Slavery in Ancient Greece and Rome

Slavery in Ancient Greece and Rome

Jacqueline Dembar Greene

Watts LIBRARY

Franklin Watts
A Division of Grolier Publishing
New York • London • Hong Kong • Sydney
Danbury, Connecticut

Note to readers: Definitions for words in **bold** can be found in the Glossary at the back of this book.

Photographs ©: Archive Photos: 5 top, 25; Art Resource, NY: 33 (Giraudon), 40 (Erich Lessing), 14 (Erich Lessing/Fine Arts Archive), 11 (Werner Forman Archive, British Museum, London); Bridgeman Art Library International Ltd., London/New York: 9 (AMQ100557/Attic red-figure bell-crater, detail showing a potter painting a bell-crater, by the Komaris Painter. Greek. Ceramic. Ashmolean Museum, Oxford, UK); Corbis-Bettmann: 45 (Baldwin H. Ward), 8, 34; North Wind Picture Archives: 5 bottom, 6, 10, 12, 16, 20, 23, 28, 30, 42, 44, 50; Superstock, Inc.: 26, 36, 38, 46; The Art Archive: 19.

Cover illustration by Carol Werner.

Visit Franklin Watts on the Internet at:
http://publishing.grolier.com

Library of Congress Cataloging-in-Publication Data

Greene, Jacqueline Dembar.
    Slavery in Ancient Greece and Rome / by Jacqueline Dembar Greene
        p.   cm.— (Watts Library)
    Includes bibliographical references and index.
    ISBN 0-531-11693-X (lib. bdg.)   0-531-16539-6 (pbk.)
    1. Slavery–Greece–History–Juvenile literature. 2. Slavery–Rome–History–Juvenile literature. 3. Civilization, Classical–Juvenile literature. [1. Slavery–Greece. 2. Slavery–Rome.] I. Title. II. Series.
HT863.G75 2000
306.3'62'0937—dc21
                                       00-038197

Contents

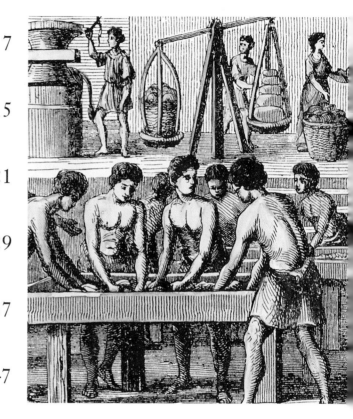

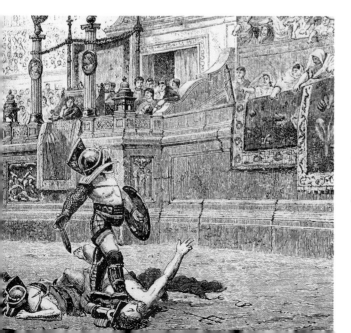

A map of ancient Greece showing the city-states

Chapter One

Society Built on Slavery

More than 2,000 years ago, along the shores of the Mediterranean and Aegean seas, many **city-states** were founded. Each territory had a large city as its center and its own government. Although they often fought each other, the people in this area spoke the same language. In earliest times, they called these lands **Hellas**, which later was named Greece. The people called themselves **Hellenes**. They called all foreigners **barbarians** and considered them inferior.

Hellas became the first society dependent on slavery for its prosperity. Most slaves were captured in wars against neighboring city-states and foreign lands. Prisoners of war, families of dead soldiers, and war orphans became slaves of the Hellenes. Slave traders traveled to distant countries, kidnapped free people, and sold them in open markets called **agoras**. Sailors, merchants, military officers, and pirates kidnapped and sold people into slavery, making high profits.

A person who was free one day could become the slave of another person overnight. Anyone convicted of a crime could be sentenced to slavery instead of jail. Some **debtors**, men who could not repay money they owed, became the slaves of wealthy men to work off their debts. Poor parents sometimes sold their children into **bondage** because they could not afford to feed them.

Prisoners of war were sold as slaves in ancient Hellas.

Variety of Slave Jobs

Ideas of democracy changed the way city-states were governed, but wealthy men ran the country and wrote its laws. The belief that slaves were inferior didn't change, and slaves were never allowed to participate in the government. They performed nearly all other tasks, however.

Slaves were an important part of a Greek family's household. In early times, most owners treated their servants kindly and shared tasks with them. However, by the ninth century B.C., Greek families wanted to buy more goods and services.

This piece of ancient Greek pottery depicts a slave painting a vase.

Instead of having their slaves work only in the household, enterprising businessmen used their slaves' labor to make large quantities of needed items, such as pottery or cloth. They sold these goods locally, as well as in other city-states and countries. As the businessmen grew wealthy, they brought in more slaves to do the manual labor. Soon, the Greeks could simply manage the businesses instead of actually doing the work.

Governments also put slaves to work. Enslaved foreigners were trained as police, tax collectors, office clerks, scribes, and executioners. Other slaves built ships, public build-

From Captives to Slaves

In 468 B.C., General Cimon of Athens captured twenty thousand prisoners. Most were sold into slavery. A few were freed after their relatives paid a ransom.

ings, and monuments. Some were forced to mine silver and gold to fill the government's treasury.

By the fifth century B.C., Greek city-states were constantly at war. Many soldiers died, and the armies needed more men. Greeks bought criminals from other countries and trained them to fight. They also used slaves to make weapons, armor, and clothing for soldiers.

Democracy for a Few

City-states in Hellas were the first civilizations in the world to base their governments on the democratic idea that all men should participate in governing. Although every citizen had the right to vote, only men over age eighteen who were sons of free parents were granted citizenship. Members of the upper class believed their time should be spent governing and discussing important ideas. They thought that any person who worked to earn a living, or was controlled or protected by another, was not worthy of citizenship. This group of people included women, foreigners, traders, peasants, laborers, and slaves.

One group of people, called **metics**, included educated foreigners working in Hellas in such businesses as banking and

the slave trade. No matter how successful they were, they couldn't vote or own land, but they had to pay taxes and serve in the army, if needed.

The Rise of Slave Markets

Large slave markets opened in Greek cities along trade routes, handling as many as one thousand slaves each day. Slave traders shouted out a slave's name, which was usually made up by the seller. They told the slave's age and background, emphasizing any special skills or qualities, and disclosed any physical problems the slave might have. Buyers inspected naked slaves on a wooden platform.

In modern money, slaves cost as little as $50 or as much as $1,000. **Artisans**, skilled craftsmen who worked with their

Selling slaves at the slave market

Salt for Slaves

Merchants traded salt for slaves. An inexpensive slave was called a "salting." A dependable slave was said to be "worth his salt."

hands, brought high prices, but slaves with education and business experience were most valuable. Slaves sold to work in mines went for a moderate price because their work conditions were so harsh that they weren't expected to live long. People who were old or weak were sold cheaply. Children also cost very little. They couldn't do much work and had to be fed, clothed, housed, and trained. Still, some masters purchased children and sold them at a profit when they were older. The government collected a tax on the price paid for each slave.

Noncitizens Do the Work

Greek citizens owned slaves partly because they believed physical labor was unhealthy. Wealthy citizens often lived in the city and owned large farming estates in the countryside. An educated slave managed the farm and acted as overseer to other slaves who worked in the fields. The owner rarely even visited.

Business owners used slaves to manage the daily operations, as well as to make the products that were sold. Sometimes, a citizen established a business for a well-educated slave but never worked there himself. The master kept most of the profits and paid the slave a small amount. Some of these slaves eventually saved enough money to buy their freedom.

Just below the upper-class Greek citizens was a large middle class. This class was made up of **freemen** who weren't afraid of physical labor or handling money. Because they worked for a living, nearly all were denied citizenship. These workers owned most of the small crafts shops, sailed the seas as merchants and traders, or ran the banks. They were essential to Greek society, but citizens looked down on them. Even educated professionals, such as doctors, lawyers, and teachers, were not always respected because they worked for pay.

On small farms, freemen worked their fields or tended livestock. These peasants also were not granted citizenship. They usually worked alone or with their families and sometimes hired a laborer or two. Few could afford to own a slave because feeding a slave was too expensive.

Time Off

Workers in Greece never had official vacations, but everyone had about sixty public holidays free from work each year.

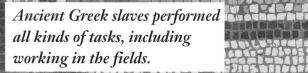

Ancient Greek slaves performed all kinds of tasks, including working in the fields.

Chapter Two

Slave Life in Greece

Slaves performed nearly every task in Greek life. They wove cloth and made clothing and sandals. They grew fruits and vegetables, made clay pots, and cooked and served meals. Some were artists who created jewelry, statues, and paintings. Others made armor and weapons.

Most slaves worked in the household. The average Greek home kept three slaves. The wealthiest homeowners had as many as fifty slaves, with one favored slave serving as manager. Loyal servants were clothed and fed fairly well, and many owners provided them with an education.

Showing Off Extra Slaves

Some wealthy men created jobs for slaves to just impress others. For example, some male slaves accompanied their masters or mistresses when they walked along the streets. One slave might only prepare his master's bath each day, whereas another would stand by to fill the master's wineglass during meals. Many households kept **pedagogues**, educated slaves who taught a master's small children at home. When the children were old enough, the pedagogue walked them to school and waited for them until the end of the day.

This illustration of ancient Greek students was copied from a vase.

While a modest household had one slave who cooked the family's meals, a wealthy man might own a master chef, bakers, a pastry cook, and several kitchen helpers. Slaves also served as doormen, valets, nursemaids, porters, and messengers.

Customs and Laws

Many customs governed how a slave could live and what he could earn. Household slaves lived with their masters and generally earned nothing. Slaves who worked in government jobs received a small wage, lived apart from their masters, and could marry and have families. Many of them received gifts of money or food from those they assisted. In rare cases, slaves who were bankers, teachers, or doctors achieved such great success that the state granted them freedom and even citizenship.

Citizens were expected to keep their household slaves for life, even if the slaves became too old or too sick to work. A master could free a slave in his will, but like other valuable possessions, most slaves were left to family members along with other property.

Some protection was available for a slave who was mistreated. A master could punish his slave for any reason, but a slave who was treated cruelly could seek help at a religious temple. If priests decided an owner's treatment was too harsh, he had to sell the slave. It was against the law to kill a servant or punish another person's slave.

Slaves in the Mines

Of all the jobs a slave might be assigned, none were worse than working in Greece's mines. The availability of vast numbers of slaves meant Greece had no reason to develop machinery to make mining easier or to use fewer workers. Mines operated 24 hours a day, and 20,000 to 30,000 male and female slaves worked 10-hour shifts under horrible conditions. Few lived long.

Miners were given little rest and small portions of food. They often became ill from overwork, accidents, and breathing

Passing On

The Greek philosopher Plato left five household slaves to others in his will. Another philosopher, Aristotle, bequeathed fourteen slaves.

in dust and fumes. Slaves who worked underground crawled through narrow shafts. They had to lie on their stomachs in a space about 36 inches (91 centimeters) tall and 24 inches (61 cm) wide and dig with a pick and a shovel.

Foremen, who sometimes were also slaves, whipped any worker who slowed down. Slaves who tried to run away rarely succeeded. When these miners were caught, their foreheads were branded with a hot iron, and they were kept in shackles.

Paths to Freedom

A slave might regain freedom in a few ways. Besides being freed in a master's will, a slave might be freed as a reward for special service. Occasionally, a slave saved his small earnings until he could buy his own freedom. Freeing a slave was called **manumission**. This occasion was marked by a solemn public ceremony usually held at a temple with many guests.

Greek priests sometimes purchased a large number of slaves and freed them to encourage manumission by others. Still, slavery continued. In desperation, many slaves tried to escape, but it was difficult. Treaties between Greek city-states provided for the return of runaways. A recaptured slave was placed in chains and sometimes branded.

Former slaves were called **freedmen**. They were not citizens. They often held low-paying jobs, but they could choose where to live and work. Some became foremen, overseeing other slaves. Others worked in professions such as banking or business.

The Philosophers' View

Most Greeks would not enslave another Greek, but they believed that foreigners were fit only for serving and following orders. At the end of the fourth century B.C., the philosopher Plato wrote that all foreigners were barbarians and that freed slaves shouldn't be granted citizenship. Plato's most famous pupil, Aristotle, said owners should treat slaves kindly, but he believed Greek society would collapse without slavery.

Eventually, some philosophers argued that all people were born free and that slavery went against nature. Euripides wrote dramas showing sympathy for enslaved prisoners of war. By 310 B.C., many Greeks began to feel uncomfortable holding a person in bondage, and numerous slaves were freed. Hiring workers seemed cheaper than buying a slave and supporting him throughout his life. People began to speak openly of freeing all slaves.

As the argument against slavery grew stronger, civil wars broke out between wealthy slave owners and free men who weren't citizens. These battles weakened Greece and left it unable to defend itself against stronger enemies. By the second century B.C., Greece was easily conquered by the growing Roman Empire.

Aristotle and Plato teach students at the School of Athens.

19

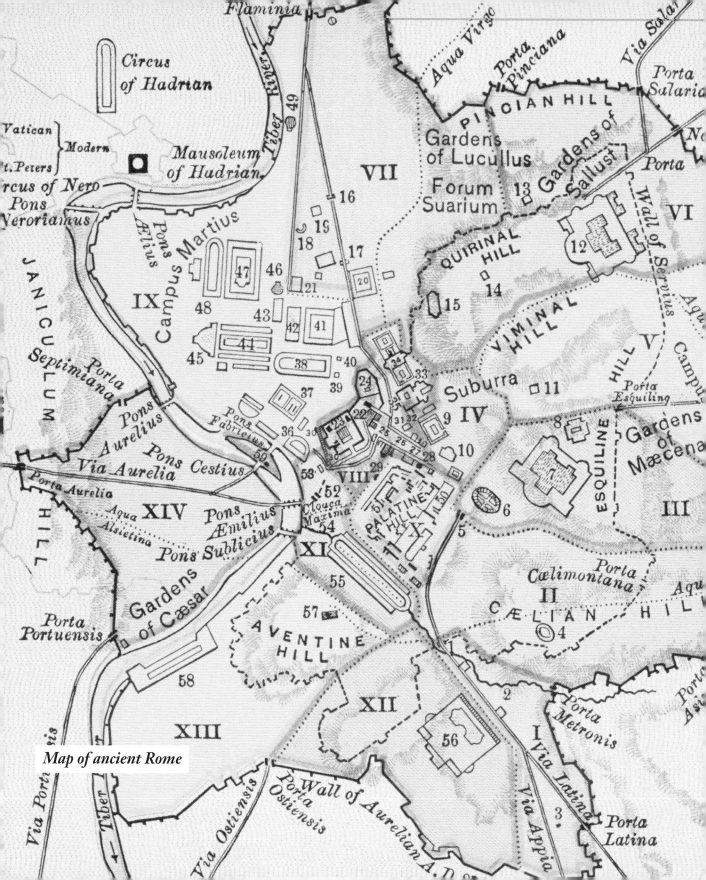

Map of ancient Rome

Chapter Three

The Rise of Roman Slavery

Around 1000 B.C., the city of Rome was founded on the Tiber River. By 44 B.C., Rome ruled the entire Mediterranean world, extending its empire as far west as Great Britain and as far east as Palestine. Rome enslaved many of the Greek people and forced each city-state to provide soldiers for the Roman army.

Rulers, Workers, and Slaves

Heads of landowning families, called **patricians**, became the politicians and rulers who made Roman laws. **Plebeians** were citizens who worked as farmers, artisans, businessmen, and traders. They had the right to vote and to serve in the army. They could also be elected to office in one of the lower assemblies of the Roman Senate. Slaves made up the lowest class. As noncitizens, they couldn't vote or hold office, and they had no control over their lives.

In Rome's early days only the wealthiest families owned slaves. As the Roman army conquered more lands, however, slaves became plentiful. Their value dropped, and plebeians could afford to buy them. The number of slaves in the empire grew, and Rome became a center for the slave trade.

Slaves from War or Trade

Instead of feeling sympathy for those they enslaved, the Romans thought prisoners of war should be grateful to be alive. Roman generals marched their military units, called **legions**, into battle, trailed by slave traders. After a city lay in ruins, the victorious general sold hundreds of thousands of captives to the slave traders, pocketing huge profits. Military officers and soldiers kept some prisoners as personal servants. The rest were marched away in chains, to be sold in cities along the route.

As trade with Africa increased, Romans bought marble, ivory, and rare spices. They also bought black slaves. From the northern countries, such as Germany, wealthy Romans purchased luxurious furs, amber stones, and white slaves.

Slaves for Sale

In Rome, as in Greece, many slaves were put to work in government and temple jobs, but most faced the terrifying prospect of standing on the auction block. They were prodded and poked by prospective buyers and bid for like cattle.

A family of slaves is sold in a Roman slave market.

Slaves were auctioned in market squares. New captives' feet were whitened with chalk, and signs around their necks listed their names and ages. Usually, the slave dealer gave each prisoner a name that described a special quality or skill. A painted mural found in the ruins of the city of Pompeii shows a slave girl standing on the auction block holding a parchment paper listing her qualities.

The auctioneer led a slave forward and asked for bids. Sometimes the seller removed the slave's one-piece garment, and prospective buyers squeezed a slave's arms and legs to test the muscle strength. Often they forced captives to run, jump up and down, or lift heavy objects to see how strong and healthy they were.

A written contract guaranteed that a slave was in good health and recorded name, age, and any birthmarks or special identifying features. If anything on the contract proved false, the buyer could collect twice the purchase price from the dealer.

By the first century A.D., some Roman rulers owned as many as twenty thousand slaves, and some wealthy men kept more than four hundred in their households.

Piracy on the Seas

Free people traveling on ships were often captured by pirates and sold into slavery. Piracy began to increase under the Romans because they wanted more slaves, and bought them without asking questions. Pirates built fast ships and secure

Conquered soldiers, now slaves, unload looted Greek artworks brought back to Rome.

Julius Caesar Taken Captive

In 76 B.C., young Julius Caesar, who later became ruler of the Roman Empire, was captured by pirates while sailing to the island of Rhodes to study law. He was imprisoned in a pirate fortress, where he spent his time writing poetry and reading it out loud to his captors. When told he would be ransomed for 20 talents, equal to nearly $100,000 in modern money, he pretended to be insulted at the low ransom set for his release. He bragged he was worth at least 50 talents. The larger sum was raised, and Caesar was released. He promptly returned to Rome, raised a huge army, and attacked his former captors. After their defeat, Caesar took back the ransom money, as well as the vast sums stored in the pirate fortress.

fortresses where they could hide. Their attacks on ships disrupted the export and import of food, and passengers were afraid to travel. Soon pirates began invading coastal towns as well as boarding ships.

Romans tried to end the attacks, but their armies suffered one defeat after another. Pirates had more than one thousand well-armed ships, manned by battle-hungry crews. They often captured Roman diplomats and nobles and ransomed them for a higher sum than they might earn by selling them as slaves.

Eventually, the Roman general Pompey attacked the pirates at sea and in their fortresses. As many as ten thousand were killed, their ships captured or burned, and their prisoners released. With the end of the pirate raids, fewer slaves reached Rome's auction blocks. To maintain enough servants, slaveholders kept all slaves born into their ownership and purchased abandoned children, criminals, and African slaves captured in tribal wars.

Slaves assist their mistress with bathing and getting dressed.

Chapter Four

Life After the Auction

A master's personality and a slave's job controlled the quality of that slave's life. Some Romans allowed their slaves to choose a spouse and raise a family, although their children became the master's property. The owner provided only basic food and clothing. The average slave received one shirt and one cloak each year, and a pair of wooden shoes every other year. Many owners treated their slaves like machines, meant to work until they broke down. These masters had no personal feelings for their slaves and punished them severely, even for small misdeeds, such as refilling a wineglass too slowly. When a slave grew old or sick, his owner might sell or abandon him.

However, some owners and slaves developed close bonds of affection. Occasionally, an owner granted his slave freedom so that he could legally marry her. Slaves who served as nursemaids often remained affectionate companions to a child throughout life. Slaves sometimes risked their lives to save their master or accompanied him into exile if he was banished for committing a crime.

A Slave's Life

While the owners slept, slaves rose before dawn and traveled to the community ovens to bake the family's bread. Kitchen slaves prepared a breakfast of boiled eggs, hot bread, fruits, and nuts, and carried it to their master or mistress. Others laid

Slaves working in a Roman bakery

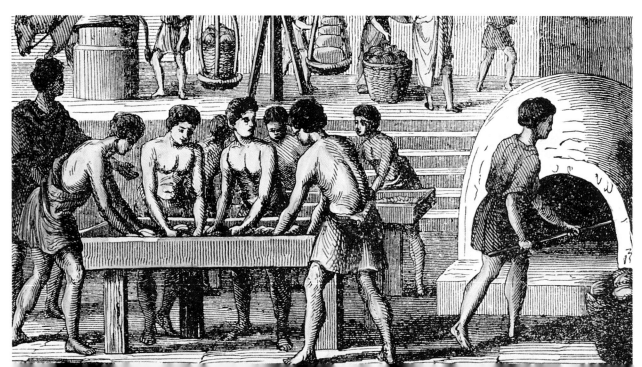

out their owners' clothes, helped them bathe and dress, and stood by as they ate.

Household slaves sewed the family's clothes or served as hairdressers, doctors, secretaries, and accountants. Masters used young slave boys dressed in fine clothes to open the door for guests, take a visitor's cloak, or pour wine. A citizen often traveled Rome's streets with a parade of slaves following behind. At night, slaves held torches to light his way. Some rich Romans didn't walk at all. Instead, several strong slaves carried them in special enclosed chairs.

In Rome, as in Greece, slaves sent to work in mines suffered the most and lived the shortest lives. Men, women, and children worked alongside convicted criminals. Young children crawled through narrow spaces in mine shafts, collecting loose mineral rocks called **ore**. Most adult mine workers were chained and forced to work naked. The slightest slowdown brought a whiplash from guards. Many of these slaves wished for death to end their suffering, and some committed suicide.

Slaves for Entertainment and Art

Romans enjoyed all types of performances, but only considered slaves fit to be entertainers. Any free person who acted in a performance lost his citizenship. Women were not allowed onstage, so men played all the female roles. Nearly all entertainers in the Roman Empire were slaves, including actors, singers, circus clowns, acrobats, and musicians.

The first theater was built in Rome in 145 B.C. It featured rows of seats in a semicircle around a stage. All performances were free. Women could attend, but had to sit in the last rows. Slaves stood in the back.

Romans loved large choruses and orchestra music, and talented slaves trained with well-known slave singers, musicians, or composers. The emperor sponsored musical competitions and awarded a laurel wreath to the winners.

Public baths were a popular gathering place. The baths had social halls where slaves served refreshments, entertained, or assisted at gambling tables. Hundreds of government slaves worked in their steam rooms, swimming pools, and cold and hot baths. Some gave massages with fragrant oils.

Romans collected and appreciated all types of art, but artists received no respect. Patricians felt that creating art was a menial task reserved for the lower class. Shops staffed by poorly paid freedmen and slaves worked in assembly-line fashion, with each worker contributing one detail to an object. One slave might make glass eyes for statues, while others specialized in painting one design, such as flowers, animals, or leaves. Because most artworks were the product of many hands, artists didn't sign them.

Agricultural Estates

Wealthy noblemen bought many small farms and combined them to create huge agricultural estates worked by hundreds of slaves. Each farm specialized in one product, such as olives

Estate Slaves

Estate slaves grew so numerous that Emperor Julius Caesar decreed that one-third of all workers on a farm must be freemen.

or grapes. Ranches had vast herds of cows, sheep, or goats.

While the master lived in the city, his slaves tended the fields or cared for the livestock, and a few trusted slaves acted as overseers. A slave on such an estate might work his entire life and never see his owner.

Farm slaves were branded like livestock and housed in special slave quarters. A prison on each estate held slaves punished for breaking rules or trying to escape. Many worked in chains and received little food or rest. The master's only concern was profits.

This mosaic shows slaves producing olive oil by pressing olives.

Holiday Celebrations

Romans celebrated more than one hundred holidays each year. Most holidays featured feasts and celebrations, although a few were solemn religious observances. A master could grant his slaves the holiday off if he chose to do so.

In December, a popular festival called Saturnalia celebrated Saturn, the god of agriculture. On this day, masters and slaves

Saturnalia, an ancient festival, was celebrated from December 17 to 24 and consisted of wild merrymaking.

exchanged small gifts, and household slaves ate with their owners. A slave might give his master a simple order, which the master obeyed with good humor.

No Escape from Slavery

To keep slaves from escaping, some owners branded their slaves' faces. Other slaves were forced to wear metal collars engraved with their owner's name. If a slave escaped, a town crier walked through the streets announcing a reward for his return. Recaptured slaves were severely punished. Some worked in chains for the rest of their lives. Others were beaten. The cruelest fate was **crucifixion**, when a slave was nailed or tied to a wooden cross and left to die.

Some slaves plotted to kill a cruel master, but it was dangerous. Roman law decreed that if a slave murdered his owner, every slave in the household must be put to death. Although rare, a slave might poison his master and not be discovered, or slaves might kill an owner on a lonely road and escape.

Paths to Freedom

It was easier to earn freedom in Rome than in Greece. If a slave saved the amount of money it would take to replace him, he could pay that sum to his owner and be set free. Some masters even gave slaves an allowance, set them up in business, or let them work for others. Masters often allowed slaves to pay a portion of their value and work off the rest.

A few owners granted freedom as a reward for special service or for years of faithful work. Female slaves might be freed after they had several children, which the master kept. Some owners freed their slaves so that they wouldn't have to continue to feed and clothe them. Upon his death, an owner could free one or many of his slaves in his will.

At times, the government freed a slave as a reward for reporting a crime or capturing a criminal. But under Roman law, a freed slave was not granted citizenship. The child of a freed slave was the first in his family born into Roman citizenship.

By 30 B.C., about 400,000 slaves lived in the city of Rome and made up half of its population. In all of Italy, there were nearly 1.5 million slaves. More and more owners freed their slaves and hired them to work when needed. Emperor Augustus became afraid that too many slaves would depend on state charity to survive. He ruled that no master could free more than one hundred slaves, but he placed no limit on how many slaves a master could own.

This photo shows the ruins of Rome's ancient Colosseum

Chapter Five

Let the Games Begin

Gladiator games, in which trained men fought against each other or battled wild animals, were made popular by the Romans. Gladiator comes from the Latin word *gladius*, meaning "sword." As their popularity grew, games were held about 175 times each year, lasting from a day to as long as a week. Romans built great **amphitheaters**, immense round buildings with tiers of seats for spectators and an arena at the center where fights

The Greatest Amphitheater

The Colosseum was built in Rome by emperors Vespasian and Titus in A.D. 80 to present gladiator games. It held 50,000 spectators.

In the center of the Colosseum, there were holding cells for animals and prisoners awaiting their turn in the arena.

were held. The games had no admission charge, and they were open to all free men and women.

At first, the government forced prisoners of war, recaptured slaves, and criminals to fight in reenactments of battles. Although they were called games, these were actual battles, and men fought for their lives with real weapons. Many died. The emperor often granted freedom to survivors.

Romans thought the games were kinder than other forms of punishment for criminals sentenced to death. Citizens also thought the fear of becoming a gladiator might prevent some men from committing serious crimes.

Only a few Romans wrote or spoke against the cruelty of the games. Marcus Cicero, a statesman and philosopher, questioned how violence and bloodshed could be considered entertainment. Lucius Seneca, another famous philosopher, expressed shock at the idea of humans killing each other for sport. Yet thousands filled the arenas, cheering their favorite gladiators.

How Gladiators Were Trained

Several rigorous schools trained gladiators. Trainees had to swear to endure hardship and wounds without complaining. Their training, diet, and sleep schedule were controlled. Anyone who broke the rules was whipped, branded, or put in chains.

Gladiators trained in different categories, depending on the weapons they used. They fought with daggers and nets or with swords and shields. Some held one sword in each hand, and others used slingshots. Others fought while riding horses or driving chariots. Fighters for each match were chosen at random, and gladiators with different kinds of weapons often fought each other.

Gladiators in training

The night before a game, a lavish feast was held for the fighters. Some ate and drank and celebrated what might be their last night in this world. Others sat alone or said their last good-byes to their families.

Entertainment for the Citizens

When the games opened, gladiators paraded into the arena, followed by servants bearing their weapons. The fighters stopped in front of the emperor's gilded box and shouted together, "Those who are about to die salute thee!"

The emperor, with his empress beside him, sat on a throne surrounded by his family, friends, and servants. Officials and diplomats sat on marble seats under the shade of retractable awnings. Fountains sprayed perfumed water to cool the air. Throngs of spectators bought food and drinks, listened to bands that played during breaks or at exciting moments in the games, and scrambled for gifts and sweets that the emperor had servants toss into the crowd. Blaring trumpets echoed through the noisy arena to announce each fight.

Fighting to Live

Gladiators fought each other until one, or both, died. Sometimes, when two gladiators battled to a tie, the fight was stopped, and the emperor decided the men's fate. The crowd roared its feelings, waving handkerchiefs or holding their thumbs up if they wanted a brave gladiator to be spared. The emperor signaled his decision by holding his thumb up (for life) or down (for death). When he ruled death for a gladiator, the fighter's opponent dealt the final blow. There was also an official who could decide the match. A losing gladiator could kneel and raise his arm and the official often spared him.

At some events, a gladiator was forced to fight a new opponent each time he won, until finally his strength failed, and he was killed. At the end of each bloody battle, slaves carried off the dead and spread fresh sand on the arena floor. In fact, the word arena from the latin word *harena*, meaning "sand."

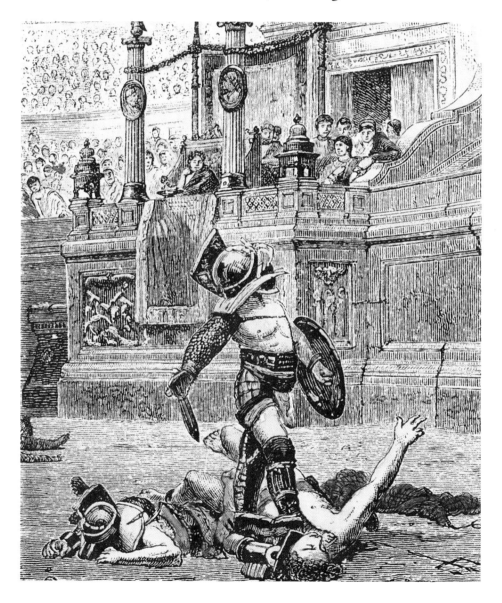

A Roman gladiator awaits the decision to spare or kill his opponent.

Gladiators led brutal lives, and a few committed suicide to end their suffering. Yet some liked the violent life. They petitioned the emperor to hold the events more often. A small number of gladiators gained fame, and spectators placed bets on their success. Sculptors carved statues of them. Poets wrote of their bravery, and adoring fans showered them with gifts and money. Some gladiators were free men who fought for fortune and glory. But free men could quit whenever they wished, unlike gladiators who were slaves.

If a slave gladiator survived three years in the arena, he was released to serve as a bodyguard, assist an army officer, or perform staged fights. After two more years, he gained his freedom. The best gladiators earned enough money from gifts to purchase their freedom. Some were pardoned by an emperor and received a symbolic wooden sword as a tribute. No matter how great a gladiator's skills, unless he gained freedom, his victory might last only until he met his next opponent.

Androcles and the Lion

Romans told a story of a runaway slave named Androcles who came upon a wounded lion and removed a thorn from the animal's paw. When Androcles was recaptured, he was thrown into the arena to fight a wild animal. As he cowered in the ring, waiting to die, he found his opponent was the same lion he had helped. The lion refused to attack, and the emperor granted Androcles his freedom. It was said that he traveled the country displaying the tame lion and telling his astonishing story.

A gladiator fights for his life against a hungry lion.

Animals in the Arena

Highlights of the games were battles between men and wild animals. Gladiators wore animal skins and stepped into the arena to fight roaring, hungry beasts, such as lions, tigers, and leopards.

Sometimes the games opened with a display of animals from distant lands. Many Romans had never seen giraffes, elephants, zebras, gorillas, bears, or ostriches and other exotic birds. Trainers dressed some of the animals in costumes and taught them tricks. Others animals were pitted against each other or were hunted in the arena by gladiators with spears or arrows. Very few of the animals lived long.

The Revolt of Spartacus

Spartacus was a slave who led a revolt of seventy fellow gladiators in 73 B.C. The men stole kitchen knives and overpowered their guards. They fled to Mount Vesuvius. When other slaves in Italy heard of the revolt, they escaped and joined the band of gladiators. Eventually, 120,000 slaves fought for their freedom under Spartacus's command, holding off Roman army attacks for two years. Spartacus was finally defeated by eight Roman legions and probably died during the battle. Thousands of his recaptured men were crucified along the road to Rome as a warning to others.

Pope Gregory the Great

Chapter Six

The Fall of Roman Slavery

Most Romans considered slavery to be a natural part of life. Priests of most ancient religions, as well as the growing Christian Church, shared this belief. The early Roman Church welcomed converted slaves but didn't try to gain their freedom. Jesus preached that a good slave should work hard for his master. Peter, one of the twelve apostles, advised slaves to subject themselves willingly to their masters' wishes. Augustine, who was made a saint after his death, wrote that a slave's condition was ordained by God.

Pope Gregory I (A.D. 590 to 604), who owned hundreds of slaves, ruled that no slave could become a priest or marry a free Christian. Bishops could not free a church slave unless they personally paid his replacement value. In A.D. 630, the Church decreed that no runaway slave could receive Communion.

Gains in Equality

Eventually, the Church recognized the inhumanity of slavery. Priests urged Christian masters to free their slaves as an act of charity. Politicians, lawyers, judges, and others urged that all human beings should be treated as equals. A group of philosophers called the Stoics wrote that all men were born equal under the eyes of God.

As the Roman Empire became weaker, it lost battles, land, and its source of foreign slaves. With fewer captives available, slave prices rose sharply. Even wealthy owners couldn't afford as many slaves. Those with modest incomes could rarely afford any. It became cheaper to hire free men than to support a slave for a lifetime. By the fourth century A.D., nearly all miners, artisans, and farmers were free men who were hired and paid for their work.

Overpopulation in the cities led to outbreaks of disease. Many people died, and others left to seek a safer life in the countryside. With fewer people in the cities, large farms couldn't sell all their products. Estate owners broke up their holdings, giving slaves their freedom and renting land to them in exchange for a portion of the crops they grew.

After dominating the world for centuries, the Roman Empire finally collapsed in the fifth century A.D. Its system of slavery ended, gradually replaced by the **manor system**, in which wealthy landowners rented small farms to free men called **serfs**.

Democracy and Slavery in the Americas

Centuries later, the influence of Rome and Greece spread to newly discovered lands. European explorers carried with them the deeply rooted ideas that foreigners were inferior and were destined to be slaves. As in ancient Greece, many people believed in the ideas of democracy but didn't see the contradiction of enslaving the people whom they conquered.

As the American colonies were established, the plantation system reflected the old practices of large Roman agricultural estates. Foreign slaves purchased on the auction block farmed huge tracts of land. They were housed in slave quarters and sometimes kept in chains. Slaves were punished harshly for breaking the smallest rules. They were treated as property until they died, often from mistreatment and overwork. Children born to slaves became the property of the masters; families were often separated and sold to different owners; and runaways were severely punished or killed.

Rich men are served by their slaves.

The Greek idea that there could be democracy without equality for everyone persisted. Wealthy landowners believed a successful man was rich enough not to perform any labor but to have slaves do these tasks while he spent his time writing, thinking, and governing. Many people believed there was no way to run a successful and prosperous plantation other than to use slave labor. Slaves were not considered fit to vote, hold office, serve in the army, or choose legal marriage.

As in Rome, slavery in the Americas lasted until enough people saw the inhumanity of treating others as lesser human beings. Civil strife and the failure of building a society on slavery weakened Greece and Rome, but slavery died slowly and hard in the ancient world.

Timeline

Greece
B.C.

750 to 650	The Greeks settle the Thracian peninsula.
483	Silver mines open using slave labor.
480 to 399	The Golden Age of Greece begins.
477	Athens rises to power.
447 to 431	The Parthenon is built.
404	Sparta rises to power.
399	Socrates is condemned to death.
310 to 300	The number of slave manumissions increases significantly.
146	Rome conquers Greece.

Rome
B.C.

Circa 1000	The city of Rome is founded.
509	The Roman Republic is established.
272	Roman armies conquer the entire Italian peninsula.
264	The first gladiator games are held in Rome.
146	Rome conquers Greece.
145	The first Roman theater is built.

139	Slaves in Sicily revolt.
104	A second slave revolt occurs in Sicily.
76	Young Julius Caesar is captured by pirates.
73 to 71	Spartacus leads a slave revolt.
66 to 63	General Pompey defeats pirates in the Mediterranean.
59	Julius Caesar becomes Consul.
58 to 51	Julius Caesar conquers Gaul (France).
44	Julius Caesar is assassinated.
30	Rome conquers Egypt.
22	Augustus Caesar forms a fire brigade manned by slaves.

Rome A.D.

14	Augustus Caesar dies.
Circa 30	Jesus dies.
43 to 46	Rome conquers Britain.
79	Mount Vesuvius erupts, destroying the city of Pompeii.
80	The Colosseum is built for gladiator games.
364	The Roman Empire is divided into two parts.
404	Gladiator fighting is banned.
476	The Roman Empire falls.

Glossary

agora—an open market located in the center of a Greek city

amphitheater—an immense round theater where Romans held gladiator games

artisan—a skilled craftsman or artist

barbarian—the name given by Greeks to all foreigners

bondage—the situation of a person who is held as a slave or a serf

city-state—a large city and its surrounding territory, under one government

crucifixion—a punishment for criminals or runaway slaves in which the victim was tied or nailed to a wooden cross until he died

debtor—someone who owed money

freedman—a former slave who had gained his or her freedom

freeman—a free person in Greece who worked for pay

gladiator—a slave or a free man who fought in the arena against other men or animals

Hellas—the Mediterranean lands occupied by several groups of people who all spoke Greek

Hellenes—the name of all Greek-speaking people who lived in Hellas

legion—a Roman military unit with up to six thousand infantry soldiers and two hundred cavalrymen

manor system—a social system in which wealthy landowners rented small plots to farmers

manumission—the public act of freeing a slave

metic—an educated foreigner who lived and worked in Greece but was denied citizenship

ore—a rock that contains metal, such as silver or iron

patrician—the head of a landowning familiey in Roman society

pedagogue—an educated slave who taught small children at home and later accompanied them to and from school

plebeian—a Roman worker who held citizenship

serf—a free farmer who rented land under the manor system

To Find Out More

Books

Burrell, Roy. *The Romans*. Oxford University Press, 1991.

Chrisp, Peter. *The Romans*. New York: Chelsea Juniors, 1994.

Clare, John D., editor. *Classical Rome*. San Diego: Harcourt Brace Jovanovich, 1993.

Corbishley, Mike. *What Do We Know About the Romans?* New York: Peter Bedrick Books, 1992.

Desramps-Leguine, Sophie and Denise Vernerey. *The Ancient Greeks, In the Land of the Gods*. Brookfield, CT: Millbrook Press, 1992.

Dineen, Jacqueline. *The Romans*. New York: New Discovery Books, 1992

Nardo, Don. *Life in Ancient Rome*. San Diego: Don Lucent Books, 1997

Pearson, Anne. *Ancient Greeks*. New York: Alfred Knopf, 1992

Schomp, Virginia. *The Ancient Greeks*. New York: Marshall Cavendish, 1996

Organizations and Online Sites

The British Museum
http://www.thebritishmuseum.ac.uk/world/world.html
Created by the British Museum in London, England, this site allows you to explore many world cultures, including Greece. You can view images of the museum's collection of ancient Greek artifacts online.

The Greeks
http://www.pbs.org/empires/thegreeks
This site, built as a companion to the PBS television series, allows visitors to learn some ancient Greek words, play with an interactive map, and discover more about the people and history of ancient Greece.

Illustrated History of the Roman Empire
http://www.roman-empire.net/children/index.html
This site provides a wealth of information on the Roman Empire including history, housing, food, and clothing.

The Metropolitan Museum of Art
1000 Fifth Avenue at 82nd Street
New York, NY 10028-0198
http://www.metmuseum.org/
The museum displays thousands of artworks and artifacts from many historical periods, including ancient Greece.

Odyssey Online
http://www.emory.edu/CARLOS/ODYSSEY/
This site provides visitors with information, images, maps, and games about ancient Greece and Rome as well as other ancient cultures.

University of Pennsylvania of Archeology and Anthropology
33rd & Spruce Streets
Philadelphia, PA 19104
http://www.upenn.edu/museum
This museum's site offers images and information on the life in ancient Greece as part of its online exhibits.

A Note on Sources

My interest in writing about slavery in Greece and Rome began with the first book I wrote for this series, *Slavery in Ancient Egypt and Mesopotamia*. I found much more information on Greece and Rome than I could use in this book. I loved learning small details of daily life in the pages of Will Durant's books, *The Life of Greece* and *Caesar and Christ*. Both of these called *The Story of Civilization*.

Writing about slavery was one of the hardest topics I ever researched. It is such a sad part of world history. But I learned to understand how people came to rely on slave labor, and how their ideas made them believe that it was the way society was meant to be. When I read about slavery in Rome, especially on large farming estates, I realized how many ancient ideas affected the way American slavery took hold in a new world. Just as in the Roman empire, it took a civil war, and many lost lives, before slavery finally ended.

—Jacqueline Dembar Greene

Index

Numbers in *italics* indicate illustrations.

About the Author

Jacqueline Dembar Greene has always been fascinated by people living in past times, and she enjoys writing about times and places that most readers know little about. She believes that the word "history" truly means "his story," and could as easily have been "her-story." She has written numerous fiction and nonfiction books describing people and places far removed from our own time. Her picture book, *Butchers and Bakers, Rabbis and Kings*, set in Tudela, Spain, in 1114 was a finalist for the National Jewish Book Award. Her historical novels, *Out of Many Waters* and *One Foot Ashore*, set in 1654, were both named Sydney Taylor Honor Books.

Ms. Greene has traveled throughout the southwestern United States, Mexico, Europe, and Russia. She has used her experiences and photographs in writing several non-fiction books for Franklin Watts, including *The Maya*, *The Chippewa*, *The Tohono O'Odham*, and *Powwow: A Good Day to Dance*.